Living in
Two Worlds

Contents

Features

What can you tell from a turtle's shell?

Visit **www.rigbyinfoquest.com**
for more about **TURTLES.**

Living in Two Worlds

Many of the world's most interesting creatures live in two worlds—in water and on land.

Many of these creatures are **amphibians**. Some are **reptiles**. Others are **mammals** that spend time in the water looking for food. Some birds and insects also spend their lives both in water and on land.

1 Dragonflies lay their eggs in water.

WORD BUILDER

The word *amphibian* comes from the Greek word *amphibios,* meaning "a being with a double life."

5 The new dragonflies fly away.

Life Cycle of Dragonflies

4 The new dragonflies dry their wings in the sun.

3 After a while, the nymphs climb out of the water. They break out of their old skin. Now they are dragonflies.

2 The young are called **nymphs.** They can take several weeks to hatch.

Frogs and Toads

Frogs and toads are amphibians. Amphibians cannot live far from a watery environment. Like most amphibians, frogs and toads lay their eggs in water. Tadpoles hatch from the eggs. Each **larva** looks like a little fish with a long tail. It takes in oxygen through its gills. Later, it develops lungs and breathes air. The tadpoles grow and change until they can live on land as well as in the water.

Don't Be Fooled

Most toads are lumpy and bumpy. They have short legs. Most frogs are shiny and smooth. They have long legs.

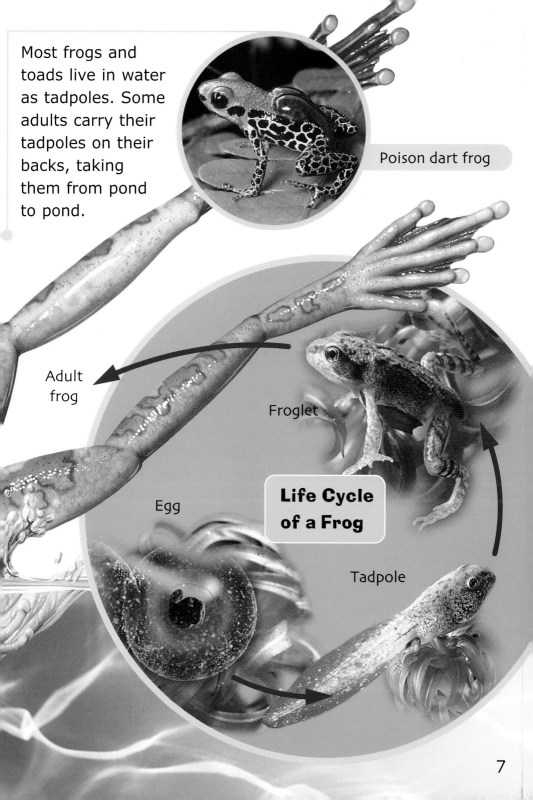

Most frogs and toads live in water as tadpoles. Some adults carry their tadpoles on their backs, taking them from pond to pond.

Poison dart frog

Adult frog

Froglet

Egg

Life Cycle of a Frog

Tadpole

7

Lizards

Lizards are reptiles. Many reptiles live on land and in water. Many lizards live near freshwater. Some search for insects in the plants that grow beside rivers and lakes. Some jump into the water to escape their enemies.

The marine iguana is the only lizard that spends time in an ocean. It dives under waves to eat plants that grow on rocks by the seashore.

South America

Marine iguanas live on the Galapagos Islands. These islands are home to many unusual and wonderful animals.

Crocodilians

Crocodiles and alligators belong to
a family of reptiles called **crocodilians.**
Crocodilians are some of the world's
largest and most dangerous reptiles.
They can float easily in water
and drift slowly toward their **prey.**
This helps them save their energy
for a surprise attack!

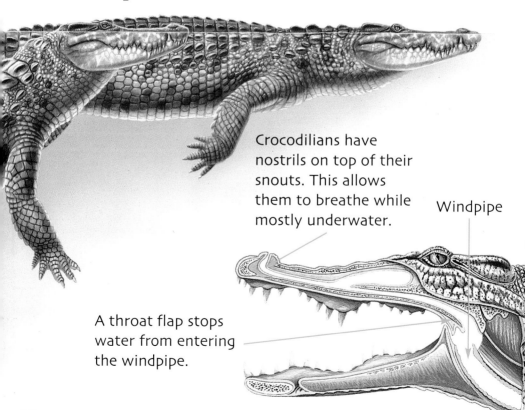

Crocodilians have
nostrils on top of their
snouts. This allows
them to breathe while
mostly underwater.

Windpipe

A throat flap stops
water from entering
the windpipe.

Crocodilians Up Close

Crocodilians have thick, scaly skin to keep them safe. Their webbed toes and long, swishing tails help them move quickly through the water. Their powerful jaws and strong, sharp teeth help them snatch and kill their prey.

Crocodilians may be fierce creatures, but the female looks after her eggs and young more than most reptiles. A mother and her young often stay together for many weeks until the hatchlings can look after themselves.

A female alligator will carry her hatchlings in her mouth to a pond, where she will look after them.

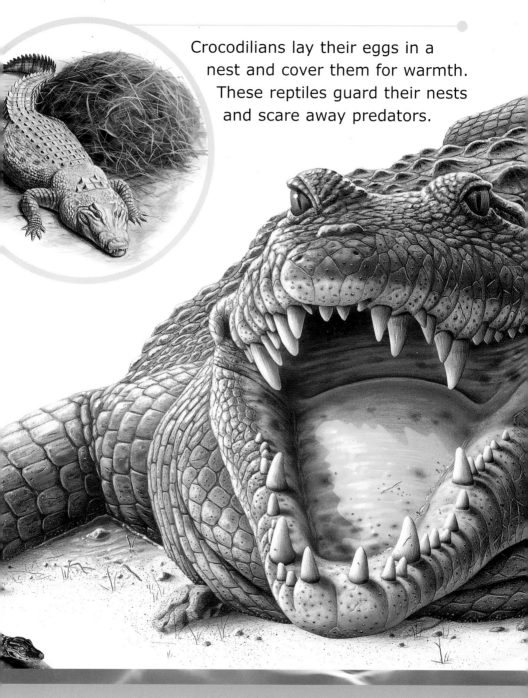

Crocodilians lay their eggs in a
nest and cover them for warmth.
These reptiles guard their nests
and scare away predators.

Crocodilians can crawl.

Central
America

The basilisk lizard from
Central America runs across
the water on its long legs. It
has scaly fringes on its back
toes that keep it from sinking.

Crocodiles and alligators live in warm, swampy countries around the world. American alligators often hunt fish around waterbird nesting sites. An alligator can leap from the water to catch a young bird.

Don't Be Fooled

Alligator

When an alligator's mouth is closed, you can see its top teeth only. An alligator has a wide snout.

Crocodile

When a crocodile's mouth is closed, you can see its top teeth and some of its bottom teeth. It has a narrower snout.

Crocodilians do not use their legs much for swimming. Instead, they use their long, strong tails as paddles to move through water.

Crocodilians can gallop.

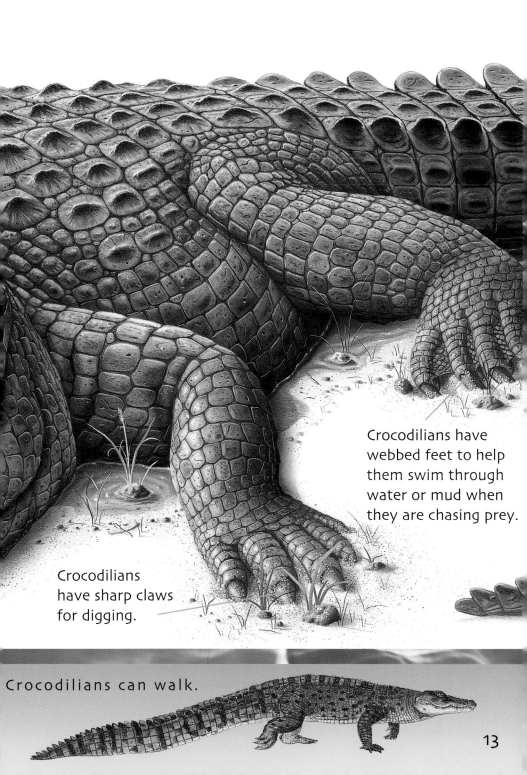

Crocodilians have webbed feet to help them swim through water or mud when they are chasing prey.

Crocodilians have sharp claws for digging.

Crocodilians can walk.

13

Turtles

Turtles are reptiles, too. Many turtles live both on land and in water. Most turtles come to the surface of the water to breathe air, but some turtles can also take in oxygen from the water.

Most freshwater turtles lay their eggs in soil or in sand. They hunt on land as well as in the water. Turtles' shells help protect them. Most turtles can pull their heads into their shells if they are in danger.

What can you tell from a turtle's shell?

Visit **www.rigbyinfoquest.com**
for more about **TURTLES.**

SITESEEING · PLANTS & ANIMALS ·

16

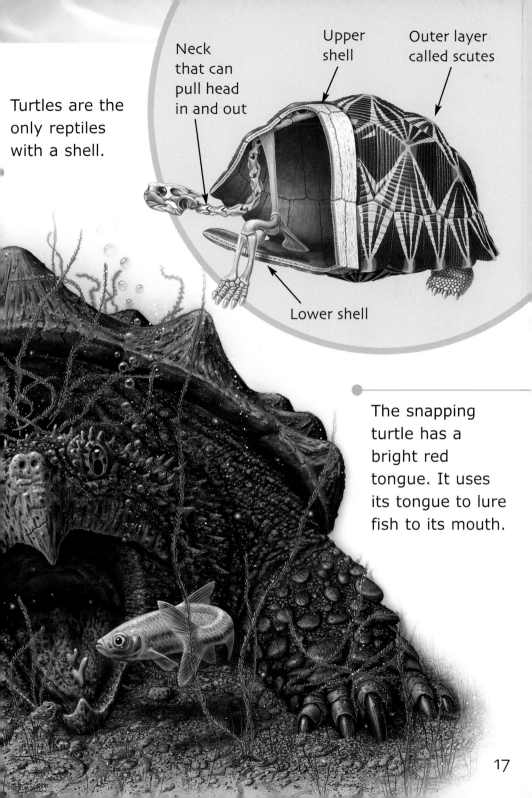

Neck that can pull head in and out

Upper shell

Outer layer called scutes

Turtles are the only reptiles with a shell.

Lower shell

The snapping turtle has a bright red tongue. It uses its tongue to lure fish to its mouth.

Furry Swimmers

Many mammals live in and out of water. Beavers, otters, and raccoons live in or near water. Some of these furry swimmers have webbed feet and a special coat to keep them warm.

Some of these animals even build their homes in the water. Beavers fell trees with their huge front teeth. They use the trunks and branches to make homes called lodges in the water.

Freshwater otters live along rivers, streams, and lakes in many parts of the world. They are expert swimmers and divers.

Raccoons live in North America. They hunt in pools and streams for frogs and fish.

Where beavers live

Trick or Truth?

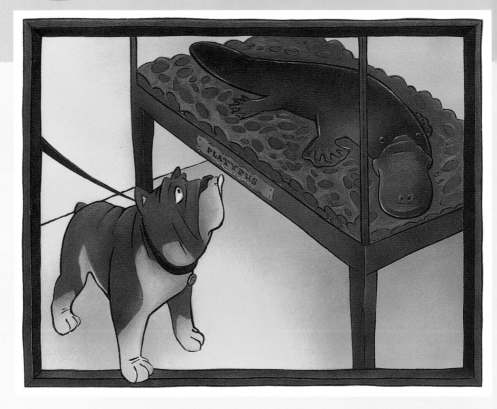

A gift from a faraway land has all sorts of Londoners mystified!

In 1798, a stuffed platypus was sent from Australia to England. The people there had never seen a platypus before. They thought it was a trick. They thought someone had stitched the bill of a duck to the body of an otter!
Was it trick or truth?

20

Strange but True!

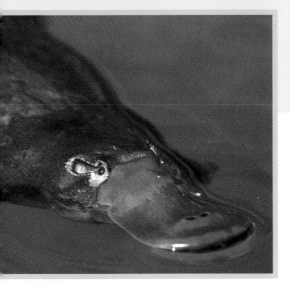

The platypus may seem a bit mixed up, but it is for real. It has a bill like a duck's and webbed feet for swimming. It is furry and about as big as a cat. It is a mammal, but it lays eggs. Baby platypuses drink their mother's milk.

Platypuses live in Australia. They dig burrows in the banks of streams. The burrows are usually underwater. The platypus is perfectly suited to living in and out of water.

The eyes and ears of the platypus are in a special groove that closes when the animal is underwater.

When on land, the platypus can fold back the webs on its front feet so it can use its claws to walk and dig.

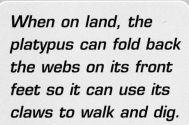

Sea Mammals

Sea lions are sea mammals. They are expert swimmers. Although they spend much time at sea, they come back to shore to have their babies, called pups. Sea lions can move well on land.

Hundreds of sea lions gather on rocky coasts in large, noisy groups called colonies. They bark, grunt, and bellow at each other.

Most sea lions live in the northern part of the world. They hunt for food such as fish, squid, and octopus in seaweed forests.

Walruses are sea mammals. They can pull themselves up onto land with their long, strong tusks.

Taking the Plunge

People also spend a lot of time in water. They swim, fish, and dive. They like to explore coral reefs and kelp forests in search of fish and other sea life. People may not have special ear or throat flaps, but they have invented many things to help them survive for long periods of time in a watery world.

Scuba diver

WORD BUILDER

The word *scuba* is made up from the first letter of five different words: **s**elf-**c**ontained **u**nderwater **b**reathing **a**pparatus.

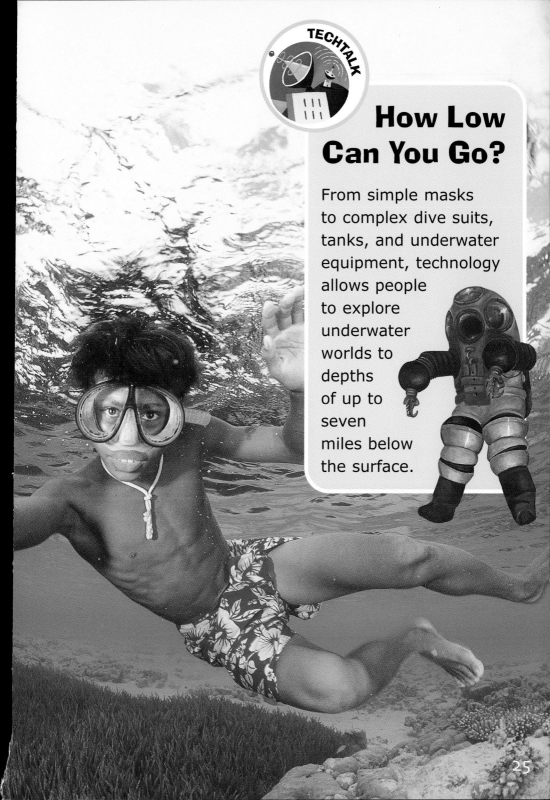

How Low Can You Go?

From simple masks to complex dive suits, tanks, and underwater equipment, technology allows people to explore underwater worlds to depths of up to seven miles below the surface.

Glossary

amphibian – (*am FIHB ee uhn*) a cold-blooded animal that lives part of its life in water and part on land. Frogs, toads, and salamanders are amphibians.

crocodilian – the name for the family of large reptiles that includes alligators and crocodiles

larva – the young, wormlike form of an animal that must grow and change a lot before it looks like its parents

mammal – an animal that feeds its young on mother's milk. Mammals are warm-blooded and are the only animals that have hair.

nymph – the newly-hatched form of some insects. A nymph must go through major body changes before it looks like an adult.

prey – an animal that is hunted and eaten by another animal

reptile – a cold-blooded animal that crawls on its belly or creeps on short legs. All reptiles have dry, scaly skin.

Index

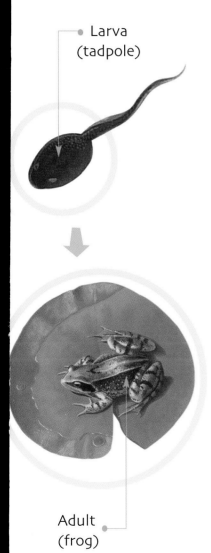

Larva
(tadpole)

Adult
(frog)

Discussion Starters

1 Some fierce animals, such as crocodilians and sharks, have a bad reputation with people. Do you think these animals are cruel or are they just fighting for survival?

2 Many turtles have shells with beautiful colors and patterns. In some places, turtles have been hunted and killed for their shells. If you saw a turtle shell for sale, what would you do?

3 Of all the animals in this book, which do you want to learn more about? Why? How will you learn more?